PETER PAUPER PRESS
Fine Books and Gifts Since 1928

OUR COMPANY

In 1928, at the age of twenty-two, Peter Beilenson began printing books on a small press in the basement of his parents' home in Larchmont, New York. Peter—and later, his wife, Edna—sought to create fine books that sold at "prices even a pauper could afford."

Today, still family owned and operated, Peter Pauper Press continues to honor our founders' legacy—and our customers' expectations—of beauty, quality, and value.

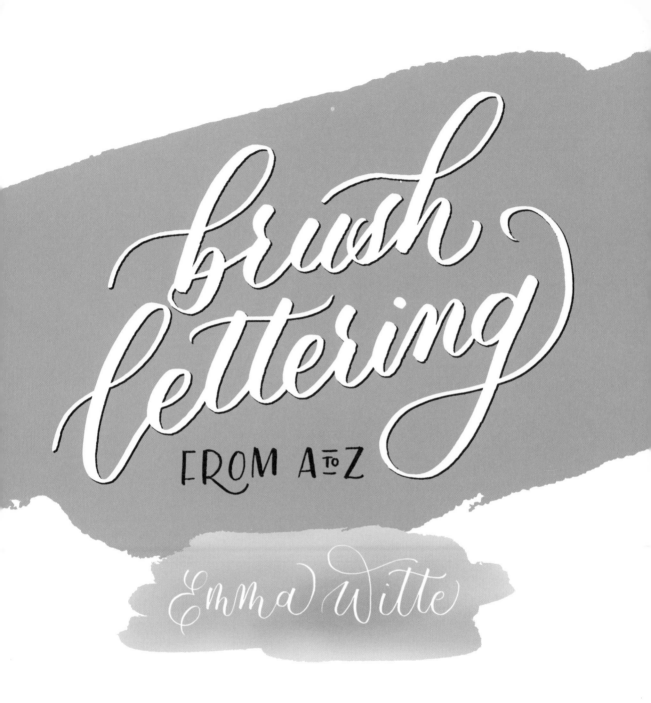

brush lettering

FROM A TO Z

Emma Witte

Peter Pauper Press, Inc.
WHITE PLAINS, NEW YORK

dedication

To anyone who picks up
this book, flicks through
a few pages and thinks,
"Nah. I can't do this—
my handwriting sucks."

This is mine,
and you can.

Designed by Heather Zschock
Text and illustrations copyright © 2018 by Emma Witte.

Published by Peter Pauper Press, Inc.
202 Mamaroneck Avenue
White Plains, New York 10601 USA

Published in the United Kingdom and Europe by Peter Pauper Press, Inc.
c/o White Pebble International
Unit 2, Plot 11 Terminus Rd.
Chichester, West Sussex PO19 8TX, UK

ISBN 978-1-4413-2707-9
Manufactured for Peter Pauper Press, Inc.
Printed in China

7 6

Visit us at www.peterpauper.com

table of contents

introduction

THERE MUST BE A
disciplined eye
AND A *wild mind.*

— DOROTHY PARKER

Hey there, pen friend! I've kicked off this book with a quote that rings true to me about what's essential for creativity: having both fun and rules. If you've never met a walking contradiction, hi! I'm Emma, and it's great to meet you.

After years of climbing the corporate ladder, working full-time while completing my bachelor's degree in business, I was bored. I liked my job, but was playing by everybody else's rules. What I did every day was predetermined. I got restless.

Brush lettering was my escape. Its rules satisfied my desire to know *how* and *why* things are done, but it also allowed immense creative freedom to break all the rules I'd learned. There is nothing more liberating than sitting down with a pen and creating something from scratch, from your mind to paper.

In our digital world, trends can dictate how everything looks, to the point where it all becomes one big generic nothing. Harnessing the power of handmade and creating something completely unique is one of the best feelings I've ever had! It's a chance to slow down, be mindful, and relax—all while making something for ourselves, which brings a huge sense of self-satisfaction.

I know you will find joy in the art of brush lettering. So let's do this!

brush lettering basics

Handwriting vs. Hand Lettering

Lettering. Hand lettering. Handwriting. Brush lettering. Brush pen lettering. Brush calligraphy. Calligraphy. Modern calligraphy. Typography. Graphic design. Brain overload.

When it comes to the art of creating beautiful letters, the terminology can get confusing. *What am I actually doing? Did I call this technique the right thing? Is this just a case of "tomayto, tomahto"? My handwriting is atrocious; can I even do lettering? Where am I?*

All valid questions, pen friend.

First: Handwriting and hand lettering are two different things. (Hooray!)

handwriting

Traditional cursive handwriting is continuous. You can write a whole word without lifting your pen off the page. If you have good penmanship, that means your handwriting is super neat, and I'm eternally jealous of you. Many types of calligraphy are technically handwriting, despite having many similarities to hand lettering.

HAND lettering

Hand lettering (and brush pen lettering) falls under the category of drawing and illustration. We are drawing strokes and shapes that we then mindfully connect to make letters and words. It is not cursive. You take the pen off the page after each stroke, piecing together individual letters bit by bit.

While handwriting and hand lettering are different things, they play nicely together! Once you develop your hand lettering abilities and get used to breaking down words and letters into strokes, then figuring out how to piece them back together, you'll find that you pay sharper attention when you are handwriting. Hand lettering teaches you to slow down, and slowing down can help your handwriting lose that doctor-esque scrawl. You can also combine the two skills to create beautiful art!

What Is Brush Pen Lettering?

brush pen LETTERING

Brush pen lettering is hand lettering using a brush pen. Brush pens are much more price-friendly and accessible tools for lettering than traditional brushes. They're small and portable, and can be carried around everywhere. You could sit on a park bench and letter in a notebook, without the hassle of carrying around an actual brush and paint or ink.

You may hear lettering terms thrown around interchangeably. Many artists define "lettering" and "calligraphy" differently, but there's plenty of crossover between these art forms.

If you ask me? I consider calligraphy something done with a dip pen and ink. For this reason, I refer to the techniques in this book as lettering.

What this Book Covers

This book dives deep into letters and how they are created, and will take you from beginner to pen wizard in no time! I will go over brush lettering tools, how to use those tools, the strokes (or lines) each letter is made of, how to connect those strokes to form letters, and how to connect letters to form words. Later chapters cover numbers, symbols, advanced techniques, and how you can use your newfound skills on fun and creative projects.

What are you waiting for? Let's do this!

materials

What You Need to Get Started

The great thing about brush pen lettering is that it's easy to get started. All you really need is a brush pen and some paper, and supplies can set you back as little as $10.

There are many types of brush pens and paper, which is great, but choosing your first supplies can be overwhelming. I've also found that art stores quite often point beginners in the wrong direction.

This list includes much-loved products that I highly recommend, but isn't exhaustive. There are lots of brands to choose from, and trial and error is usually the best way to figure out which supplies work best for you. There is no pressure to buy all of these things, but the details are included for when you want to upgrade your collection. At minimum, I recommend one small brush pen, one large brush pen, and good quality paper. But one of anything isn't that much fun, is it?

Note: The pens listed in this section are all markers. They have fabric tips instead of individual bristles. Why? Because bristle brushes are hard to learn with! They require a lot more control, so as a beginner, I recommend you master the brush marker before trying your hand (literally) at pens with bristles. You can explore brush pens with bristles on page 142.

Small Pens

Pentel Sign Brush Pen *(recommended)*

The Pentel Sign (or Touch) Brush Pens come in 12 colors and are my favorite small brush pens (though there aren't that many small pens to choose from). These tiny-tipped pens are affordable and perfect for imitating pointed pen calligraphy due to their size! But they don't last forever, and the tips can fray and begin to lose their shape quickly. Buyer beware: these pens also have a non-brush pen alternative that looks almost identical. Ensure you buy the pens that say "touch" on them and have a metallic sheen to the plastic barrel.

Tombow Fudenosuke

Another great small pen option is the Tombow Fudenosuke (and between you and me, I love it so much more than the large Tombow Dual Brush Pens). The Fudenosuke comes in hard-tipped and soft-tipped varieties, which look almost identical (dark blue barrel or black barrel). In my experience, these Tombows have a longer-lasting tip than the Pentel. They come in black ink. There is also a double-ended Tombow Fude that is black AND gray!

Large Pens

Artline Stix Brush Markers *(recommended)*

These are my number one, all-time-favorite best recommendation ever! I am yet to find a brush pen I like more than the Artline Stix. Easy to grip, juicy, long-lasting (both in ink and tip), easily accessible, budget friendly, and they just look fun. Depending where you live, they can be found in packs of 6, 10, 16, and 20. Note that Artline Stix offers three pens that all look the same: brush, bullet, and fine liner tips. Make sure you get the brush markers.

Tombow Dual Brush Pen

The social media "must have" pen. These come in 96 colors and are available either singly or in packs. Tombows have a brush pen on one end and a small rigid felt tip on the other. They also have water-based ink, so are great for blending. These pens are prone to fraying, so only use them on high-quality smooth paper. I'd recommend gaining some experience with other pens first before trying these, given their price point and delicate nature.

Micador Stylist Brush Marker

A more cost-effective version of the Tombow Dual! I personally rate this brush marker higher than the Tombow for its crisp tip and longevity. Like the Tombow, the Micador has dual ends, water-based ink, and can be easily blended with other colors in the collection (24 in total).

Ecoline Brush Pen

The most expensive brush pen I've come across, but a big favorite! These juicy brush pens come in 29 colors plus a blender pen, which are designed to mix perfectly with the 48 colors of Ecoline ink. The Ecolines have a really large, flexible brush tip. This can make them a bit trickier to master, but is a great addition to any brush letterer's kit.

Sharpie Stained

Sharpie Stained is another serious favorite of mine! This pen is designed for use on fabrics but it is beautiful on paper. Available in 8 colors, this brush pen doesn't have that permanent marker smell like other Sharpies, and like the Micador has a nice, crisp brush tip. In classic Sharpie fashion, this marker works on most surfaces, which makes it useful for tricky projects (think: shiny surfaces other pen ink wipes off).

Crayola Marker

Hang on, a *non*-brush pen on the list? Gasp! I know. I include a Crayola cone-tipped marker in all of my workshop kits. Why? The shape of the tip forces you to pick up some good habits. You'll read more about this later (on page 124), but rotating the angle of your brush pen is a fantastic habit to get into, as it will ensure you achieve the thickest thick strokes and the thinnest thin strokes. Unlike brush pens, Crayola markers do not respond to pressure, so you need to rotate the angle as you go to use their flat side for thick strokes or the very tip for thin strokes.

Paper

No matter which type of paper you choose, promise me you'll use one that is smooth! Rough printer paper or cardstock is a surefire way to fray the tips of your brush pens.

Rhodia Paper *(recommended)*

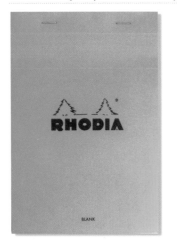

This is without a doubt the best paper for brush lettering in my opinion. You can find Rhodia notepads in a range of sizes and types, including A5, A4, A3, and plain, lined, dot grid, and lined grid. One thing I particularly love about Rhodia is that the paper is reasonably translucent, making it perfect for placing over guide sheets to give you straight lines to follow, all while still using your brush pens on high-quality paper.

Tracing Paper and Bleed-Proof Marker Pads

Any type of tracing paper will work well! It is always a little duller in color, but perfect for protecting your pens, as well as seeing through to use over your worksheets. Depending where you're from, it can be pricey. My tip is to check the kids' section of your art supply store before the art section! Bleed-proof marker pads are another alternative, usually for a similar price.

Vellum

Have you ever received a fancy invitation with a matte see-through cover? It was most likely vellum! Vellum is awesome for lettering on and can be a cheaper alternative to tracing paper.

Printer Paper

You can use regular paper if you like, but be warned: It can ruin your pens. Artline Stix markers deal with printer paper well, but I wouldn't risk other pens on it. You won't be able to achieve blending or ombré effects, as printer paper soaks up the ink too quickly. If you don't have any other alternative, try to find the highest quality, and/or smoothest printer paper.

Workspace

While brush pen lettering is portable, I recommend that you dedicate a space in your home for practice. This will get you in the zone each time you sit down, and ensure you're not hunching over your work. Check out page 16 for more info.

The Right Attitude!

I know— I bet you didn't expect me to tell you how to think or feel, but trust me. When it comes to art, we need to leave our fears and insecurities at the door. You'll make mistakes, and the sooner you accept that they are part of the process, the better. If you go in thinkiing that "practice makes progress," you will see that progress a lot quicker.

It can be discouraging to see the amazing work other artists are doing. A great quote that gets around the creative community is: "Don't compare your chapter one to someone else's chapter twenty."

Everyone is at a different stage of their creative journey. We all have natural talents and strengths, but absolutely nothing is stopping you from reaching your artistic goals. It will just require patience, practice, and accepting failure as part of growth.

Guide Sheets

Guide sheets are an important part of practice for beginners. I believe it's critical to learn the basics first, and then find your own style. If you have a solid understanding of the fundamentals, you'll be able to break the rules and find your own style while keeping your art visually appealing, coherent, and most importantly, legible.

The perfect way to start this process is with guide sheets. I encourage you to have guide sheets behind every piece of paper when you practice. This will ensure your letters and words are consistent. You already have enough to learn in the beginning. Let's not add drawing in a straight line to that list! This book includes guide sheets for practicing letters, numbers, and symbols.

Guide sheets will also assist you in creating letterforms. By tracing over the shapes and letters, you will be building the correct movements into your muscle memory, which will speed up the learning process. More on that later!

Additional Supplies

Pencil

Wait a second, lady, I thought we were doing brush lettering?

Oh, we are, pen pal. However, never underestimate the power of the pencil! Using a pencil is a great way to practice your letterforms and flex your muscle memory without the added pressure of getting perfect strokes and transitions between thick and thin lines. The pencil is also a great tool for planning layouts and practicing flourishes. A must-have! My favorite is the Staedtler Mars Technico. Unlike most mechanical pencils, which have annoyingly thin lead, this bad boy's lead is 2 mm thick! It is fantastic for light sketches. If you use a non-mechanical pencil, you'll need a sharpener.

Eraser

Personally, I don't have an eraser because I *never* make mistakes.*

Erasers are an essential addition to your toolbox, and my favorite type is the Staedtler Mars plastic eraser holder, which works a bit like a mechanical pencil. It's perfect for getting into tight spaces. I'm a lot sloppier with a traditional eraser, and tend to accidentally erase things I don't mean to!

* This is a lie.

Fine Liner / Monoline Pen

One great addition to your pen kit is a fine liner pen. My favorites are the Sakura Pigma Micron pens, which come in a range of different thicknesses and colors. They even have a brush pen range! These are high-quality pens with archival ink (meaning it won't fade over time) and are great for fauxligraphy (fake calligraphy—more about that on page 23), labeling (I like to create a swatch of different pen colors and label them with a Micron), creating thin and consistent shadow lines, or stippling. You can also use the rigid end of a Tombow Dual or Micador Brush Pen for these effects.

White Opaque Pen

If you'd like to try the highlighting technique discussed later in this book (see page 137), you will need a white opaque pen to add a white highlight to your letters. Some people prefer Gelly Rolls, but my go-to is a Uniball Signo.

Water Brush or Blender

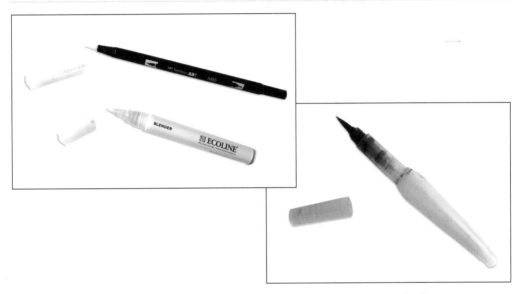

Blending different ink colors creates some really pretty results. You can do this using a water brush (a paintbrush with a hollow barrel that can hold ink or water) or a specially made blender pen. Tombow and Ecoline make blender pens, which are colorless. More info on blending later! (See page 134.)

Ruler

Rulers are very handy if you can't print or trace guide sheets. You can rule your own instead. You may need a ruler to draw faint guidelines on envelopes or other surfaces you cannot see through. You can also use them to draw fun, angled guidelines to create dynamic layouts.

Lightbox

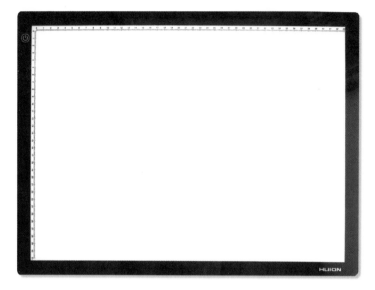

The most expensive supply in this book, but something I now cannot live without. A lightbox is a large, flat work surface that shines a bright light out of the top so that you can see through the paper you put on it. Most of them are very thin and let you adjust the level of brightness. They range from moderately to *very* costly. I use a Huion A3 lightbox that I bought from eBay. The price of these in art stores is generally quite inflated. Alternatively, you could always get creative and DIY one. Some people use their tablets with a white background, or make them using other supplies. (Look online for tutorials.)

Where to Find Supplies

One way to start: Go back to my list of recommended supplies, pick out something you'd like to try, and search online for the product name and your location to get a list of stores that stock it. It is also worth popping down to your local art store and seeing what they've got. When I started brush pen lettering, it was very difficult to find proper supplies in physical art stores. However, the art form has grown so much in popularity lately that art stores are catching up with it.

getting started

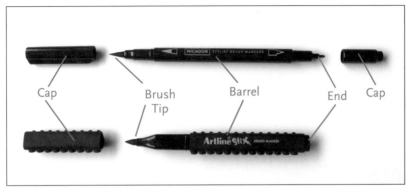

Understanding Your Brush Pen

I'm going to go out on a limb here and assume you know how to use a pencil, eraser, sharpener, and ruler. But for those of you new to the brush pen game, let's take a closer look at what they're all about. While brush pens come in many different sizes, shapes, and colors, they consist of the same parts.

Barrel

This is the thick or long part of the pen that is full of ink, and is the place you hold the pen. The Artline Stix brush marker has a designated place to hold it, as it has a tri-grip. Other pens have no such obvious place to grip, meaning it is up to you.

Brush Tip

The tip of the brush pen is the part that you apply to paper. You will use the long, flat side of the tip for thick downstrokes, and the pointy end of the tip for light upstrokes.

End

The end of a brush pen is sometimes where you may find another type of nib such as the rigid end of a Tombow Dual or Micador Brush Pen. You can also usually attach the cap to the end of your brush pen while it is in use.

Cap

The cap of the brush pen is what you remove before you use it. Always remember to put it back on when you're done to prevent it from drying out or being damaged. Be careful to put it on the right way, too. I've lost count of how many times I've given myself a heart attack by trying to force the cap back on the pen the WRONG way around. Look after those brush tips!

Handling Paper

You now know that smooth paper is the best type of paper to use, so the next most important thing you need to know about paper is that your skin can play havoc with it! Naturally, you have oils on your skin, including your hands and fingers. If you excessively touch your paper you will transfer some of those oils onto it. As you will be using smooth paper, the oils will stay on the surface, and you may find that sometimes your brush pen ink will repel from these areas, and pool up instead of flowing evenly. To ensure you don't oil up your paper too much, you can use a guard sheet. That sounds fancy, but really it is just a separate piece of scrap paper that you place under your hand and move down the page as you letter, so your hand never actually rests on the piece of paper you're lettering.

Some people go to extremes and wear cotton gloves with the thumb and first two fingers cut off. Art stores even sell them that way! Do whatever is easiest and works best for you. A piece of printer paper works fine for me.

Setting Up Your Workspace

To start, you really just need a stable surface that you can comfortably and safely sit and work at. I spent the first six months of my creative journey lettering at my dining table! Position your workstation in a well-lit area to avoid straining your eyes.

While it is taking every fiber of my being not to carry on about occupational safety, I CAN'T HELP IT. You should have all of your most-used equipment located in your optimal reach zone (within arm's length on the desk). Adjust your chair height so that your elbows form 90-degree angles when you rest your forearms on the desk. You should be able to firmly plant your feet on the floor. The best type of accessible chair has a five-star wheeled base and no arm rests! Sorry. I had to get it out.

You want your workspace to accommodate whole arm movement as you need to engage your whole arm in order to produce long letters or flourishes without having to stop and readjust. We are accustomed to just using our wrists for writing, so this will feel odd at first. Your hand should still be on the table, but lightly. Let your hand and arm graze the table top as you move it. If you hold your hand or arm *off* the table, you will find it extremely difficult to maintain control and consistency. If you plant your hand and arm in one spot, you will restrict your movement. By letting them lightly slide over the table, you'll keep your strokes consistent but allow yourself the freedom to move and create longer strokes.

Mind the GAP (Grip, Angle, Pressure)

When using brush pens, I always tell students to mind the "GAP"—a fun and easy-to-remember acronym:

G – Grip   **A** – Angle   **P** – Pressure

These are the three most important factors in brush lettering. They will differ for everyone, though, and may vary for you depending on the pen you use. Be prepared to experiment.

Grip

This is where you hold the barrel of the pen. It's totally up to you. Choose what feels comfortable and gives you the most control.

Some people find that holding a pen really close to the tip feels right, while others hold the pen about halfway up, and some even all the way towards the end! Experiment with what feels right and allows you to get the best results. You want to apply as much of the brush tip to the page as possible to get a thick downstroke, so choose a position that allows this.

Gripping too close to the brush tip will prevent you from bringing the majority of the tip in contact with the page, because your fingers get in the way.

Keep in mind that depending on which pen you use, your grip will change. A good trial activity is to draw a range of strokes on a page, varying your grip as you go. This will show you what is and isn't possible with that particular brush pen when you hold it at different positions.

Angle

Angle is the next thing to keep in mind. You don't want to hold your pen upright like an ordinary pen—this would instantly damage the brush tip when you apply pressure. Try to hold your pen at a 45-degree angle to the paper. You may not always feel comfortable doing this, but that's okay. Give it a go. When I say 45-degree angle, I don't mean 45-degree angle with the base of the brush pen pointing directly at you. Righties should lean the brush pen to the right, on a 45-degree slant, and rest the pen barrel on your knuckle, not in the webbing of your hand.

Correct

Incorrect

Correct

Incorrect

The number one thing to avoid is frayed pens. If the pen base is pointing towards you and the tip is pointing away, when you begin creating upstrokes and downstrokes, you'll be rubbing the pen on the page, fuzzing up the fabric tip. However, if you lean it over to the right, you'll drag the pen on its side down the page, which will not rub the fabric the wrong way. With the pen on its side, you'll also have a clearer view of what you're doing. Lefties should do the same thing, but to the left.

With practice, you'll also begin to change the angle of your pen mid-stroke. Why? Well, sometimes it can be very tricky to get a thin upstroke while holding the pen super flat to the page. If you adjust the angle to become more vertical as you move into an upstroke, it will be easier to achieve a thin stroke. This is particularly helpful during a transition stroke where you must go from thick to thin.

TIP: Crayola markers with conical tips are fantastic for learning this technique. Crayolas don't have a brush tip and won't respond to pressure, which forces you to rotate them as you write so that you can get the flat side on the page for a downstroke, and the very tip on the page for an upstroke. For more about this, see the **Crayligraphy** section on page 124.

Pressure

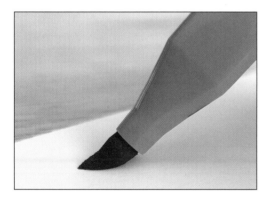 

The whole look of brush lettering revolves around contrasting thick and thin strokes, just like in most forms of calligraphy. We want our downstrokes thick and our upstrokes thin. To do this, place a fair amount of pressure on the pen when creating a downward stroke, and little to no pressure when drawing upwards.

Remember that downstrokes should be thick and heavy, and upstrokes should be thin and light. Applying the wrong pressure, or pressure on an incorrect angle, is the easiest way to damage brush pens (apart from rough paper). Make slow, mindful strokes.

Lettering for Lefties

If you're one of the (roughly) 10 percent of left-handers in the world: Firstly, hi! I hope some of you are actually reading this book and haven't put it back on the shelf thinking, "lefties can't do brush lettering!" While some techniques are different, there is absolutely nothing stopping left-handed letterers from mastering the brush pen.

Move It Around

The most important thing for any left-hander to remember is to experiment. That's not to say righties don't have to, but I think lefties face more challenges. If you're lettering on the same angle as when you write normally and it's not working for you, change it up!

Some lefties will hold their pen so that their hand and pen tip are underneath the line they are writing on, while others will curl their hand up and around. The benefit to having your hand underneath the line is that you won't smudge your work. However, this also means you won't be able to find the correct angle of the brush pen to get thick and thin contrasting strokes.

Try moving your hand so it is above the line you're lettering on, and curled over (like a mirror image of how a righty holds theirs). Many lefties hold this position but then rotate their paper to almost a landscape view in front of them, and letter on a massive angle, bringing the pen towards themselves. There is absolutely nothing wrong with this, and by lettering on the "side" and bringing your hand towards yourself, you've managed to curl your hand AND be underneath the line you're lettering on. This will prevent smudging, and ensure you're getting the correct brush tip angle.

Remember, we're just drawing shapes and connecting them. If you look at your letters and think about them more as shapes, you'll be more open to the concept of lettering on a very strange angle.

Try New Tools

I find a lot of lefties in my workshops get the hang of Crayola conic-tipped markers easily. Perhaps the rigidity of the tip better suits their hands. But if you're a lefty struggling with the very flexible brush pens, I recommend giving a Crayola a go. For more about lettering with Crayola markers, see page 124.

If you've changed your pen and paper angle and you're still experiencing some smudging, you could try using regular printer paper. This type of paper is a lot more absorbent, meaning you're less likely to smudge your work as the ink is quickly absorbed into the fibers. However, I would still recommend finding an angle that will allow you to work on smooth paper, as printer paper will not be friendly to your brush pens over time.

Sometimes beginner lefties also find it easier to learn with a smaller brush pen while they get the hang of the best angle to use. Try a Pentel Sign Pen or a Tombow Fudenosuke.

Practice Makes Progress

Like anything, the more you practice brush lettering, the better you become at it and the easier it is. This is no different for lefties. Sometimes lefties get intimidated and believe they can't do brush lettering, but it just isn't the case. Set aside some practice time each day and I guarantee you will see results. Remember, don't be afraid to adjust your grip, angle, and pressure, and/or change the pen! Two of my favorite Instagram calligraphers who nail brush lettering as lefties are @theinkyhand and @logos_calligraphy. Check them out online and *then* tell me lefties can't do brush lettering!

When you think about brush lettering, you probably don't think "pencil"! Despite the fact that we need a brush pen to create brush lettering, a pencil is an invaluable tool for learning about more advanced techniques like layouts and flourishing.

It can be frustrating to have an idea in your head, only to put brush pen to paper and create an absolute disaster. Don't believe everything you see on the internet! Those fancy, sped-up videos with perfect flourishing don't always happen naturally. I love to sketch out designs in pencil first, because it allows me to play around with the piece more and find the best possible layout for that word or quote. I can amend letter connections, create bigger or smaller loops, add flourishes and illustrations, incorporate different styles—all without wasting paper or stressing myself out.

You can also use pencils to explore and perfect a technique called **fauxligraphy**.

Step 1:

Step 2:

Fauxligraphy

The term "fauxligraphy" basically means fake calligraphy, created with a tool that does not have the natural ability to form contrasting thick and thin strokes.

Say you went to an art store and found an AMAZING pen. It was silver, glittery, and wrote as smooth as butter. The only problem was, it was a bullet tipped marker, so you couldn't use it for brush pen lettering.

This is where fauxligraphy comes in. The idea behind this technique is to "fake" the look of calligraphy and brush lettering by writing the word out in monoline (with all the lines the same thickness), then going back and manually adding the thick downstrokes that a brush pen would create naturally.

If you have a soft enough pencil as well as a nice thick pad of paper, you can get the thick / thin contrast with pencil, purely by using pressure! Obviously, the tip of a pencil isn't soft and flexible like a brush marker, and therefore won't actually create thick and thin strokes, but what it will do is draw a darker line when you apply pressure. This is a great way to work on your muscle memory by building the habit of applying pressure on a downstroke and no pressure on an upstroke. We will delve deeper into this mysterious muscle memory shortly!

Guide Sheets Explained

The best way to improve at anything is to practice. You can do that with brush lettering by using the guide sheets in this book. To ensure that you create consistent lettering, you will also use a grid. More on that in a moment!

Whether using guide sheets from this book or from another resource, the best way is to trace over them on a separate sheet of paper (such as Rhodia, which as mentioned earlier is translucent enough to see through). This is for two reasons. First, the guide sheets are most likely not printed on smooth, brush pen–friendly paper. Second, by placing another piece of paper over the top and drawing onto that, you can reuse the guide sheets again and again. The environment will thank you!

Back to the grid.

A grid is a super easy way to learn and practice lettering, to make sure your letterforms are neat and consistent. You can get as detailed as you like, including angled lines to create slanted lettering, or you can just use simple lines as below. Note: the more slanted the angle, the more formal your lettering will look.

Let's take a look at the grid in detail, as you'll be using grids throughout this book to create uniform and consistent letters. The grid below is sized for small brush pens.

There are some technical terms for all of the lines that make up the grid, and I've listed them below for your reference.

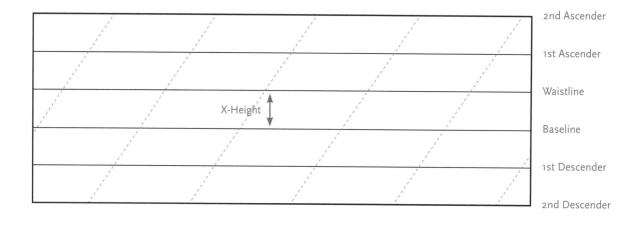

In a nutshell, the x-height is where the "body" of most of letters will sit. The ascenders and the descenders are home to our friends the ascending and descending loops (think of letters like *b* or *g* that have stems and tails). You can take your loops past the 1st ascender or descender line, but try not to let them touch the 2nd.

TIP: When the word miniscule is used, it means lowercase or small letters. When the word majuscule is used, it means uppercase or capital letters.

2nd ascender: the highest point of your stems on miniscule letters such as *d, f, l,* and *k* should not quite touch this point, but can sit between it and the 1st ascender

1st ascender: where your stems on miniscule letters such as *d, f, l,* and *k* should pass through

Waistline: the top of the body of your miniscule letters

X-Height: where the main body of your miniscule letters should be

Baseline: the bottom of the body of your miniscule letters, where the letters "sit"

1st descender: where your tails on miniscule letters such as *g, j, p,* and *y* should pass through

2nd descender: the lowest point of your tails on miniscule letters such as *g, j, p,* and *y* should not quite touch this point, but can sit between it and the 1st descender

The "bodies" of the letters in the grid will sit within the x-height, and the rest of the letters either go up or down into the ascender or descender spaces respectively, without touching the 2nd lines.

Now that you understand how the grid works, let's take things back a step and look at the staple strokes.

The guide sheets in this book are designed for small pens. For large pen guide sheets, visit www.blackchalkco.com/blbookextras.

staple strokes

What Are Staple Strokes?

You learned earlier that brush lettering is not the same as handwriting. It is drawing shapes. The cool thing about brush lettering is that the majority of the letters are all made from the same shapes, which makes it a lot easier to learn. You're probably thinking, "there's no way! The alphabet has 26 letters in it and they definitely don't all look the same." And you'd be right. The letters don't all look the same, but if you break them down into singular strokes, they have a lot of similarities.

In this book, I refer to these singular strokes as staple strokes, *staple* meaning "the main or important element of something." Every letterer or calligrapher will have a different view on what is and isn't a "staple" or "basic" stroke. Like modern calligraphy with a pointed pen, there isn't a set rule book, and it's open to interpretation.

When I began learning, I looked at other artists' interpretations of staple strokes, and I agreed with some but disagreed on others. When I began teaching, I dove deep into the content and strove to understand it in a way that I could teach to others. For me this meant creating my own interpretation of the staple strokes. I analyzed the miniscule and majuscule alphabet in detail, and these are the strokes I identified as appearing most commonly in the miniscule alphabet. There are some outliers, but don't worry about those just yet.

Familiarize yourself with the following shapes and their names:

Upstroke	Downstroke	Overturn	Underturn	Compound curve
/	/	∩	∪	∿

Left curve	Right curve	Oval	Ascending stem loop	Descending left tail loop	Descending right tail loop
C	Ɔ	O	ʃ	ʄ	ʃ

To be clear about how these strokes fit onto a lettering grid, take a look below. They are basically deconstructed letters, but we place them on the grid as we would if we were incorporating them into an actual letter. Try to imagine the letters you could make when you combine some of these strokes.

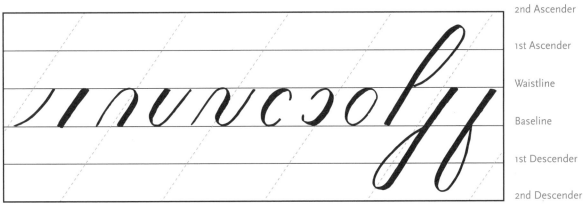

2nd Ascender

1st Ascender

Waistline

Baseline

1st Descender

2nd Descender

The Importance of Staple Strokes

Muscle Memory

In case you haven't heard of a little thing called muscle memory, let me explain. When you handwrite something, like a grocery list or a post-it note, do you have to think about how to write each letter? When you enter in your PIN at the ATM, do you have to think hard about your PIN? Most likely not. This is thanks to a friend of ours called muscle memory. When you repeat an action many times, your brain remembers it and makes your body do it, effortlessly.

You want your brain to remember the staple strokes of brush pen lettering. You don't want to have to think too hard about what you're lettering. You want it to flow magically from your mind to your pen to the paper. For this to happen, you need to build the staple strokes into your muscle memory through repetition, or "drills."

The term "drills" refers to drawing the same staple or basic strokes again and again. I can hear you from here! "That sounds boring, when do we draw letters?" Soon, my friend. There are a couple of great reasons why drills should be part of your practice.

Consistency

The aim of the game is consistency. If you wanted to have inconsistent letters, you could probably just stop reading here and figure it out yourself! But I know you don't want that. You want beautifully formed and consistent letters that are legible and look like artwork.

Drills will help you reach that level of consistency. By practicing your drills on a regular basis, you will build the shapes into your muscle memory. You will get to a point where you won't need to do drills that often, but it is crucial in the beginning to get into the habit. If you haphazardly draw random letters, it will take you far longer to learn and perfect the shapes than if you sit down every so often and draw the same shape again and again.

The reason we break letters down into staple strokes is to fast-track consistency. Imagine if your poor muscle memory had to remember 26 totally unique letters. Then, imagine if it only had to remember a handful of strokes. That's the reality here! We only have to work a few movements into our muscle memory. The rest is us piecing them together in a particular order.

If we're drawing only a handful of shapes, then theoretically our letters should end up looking consistent as can be. But that isn't always the case.

Here are some common ways letters can appear inconsistent:

• The angle of the letters changes partway through the word.

• The same stroke is drawn at different sizes in the same word.

• Guide sheets have not been used, causing problems with spacing.

By using guide sheets and paying close attention to our strokes as we draw, inconsistency can be dramatically reduced.

Speed

As a beginner, remember to take it slow. In order to reach the level of consistency that you want, you can't rush through these stages. Staple strokes are slow and deliberate movements. However, this doesn't mean you'll be slow forever. While it's key to maintain mindfulness when you draw, with practice comes speed. Building muscle memory will help you develop speed as well as consistency.

Drills

Drills will remain important for as long as you are lettering. Professional calligraphers do them too. Troubleshooting common problems is covered later (see page 154) in this book, but overcoming many of those hurdles involves practicing your drills!

You'll start by learning muscle memory from the following pages of drills, but as you become more experienced, you will use them instead as a warm up activity.

On the following pages, you will find the drills laid out as they should appear on the grid. The shape in black shows you the form and the direction it should be drawn. The gray shapes are for you to trace over, and the blank space allows you some free-hand practice space.

REMEMBER: Use a piece of high quality tracing paper, vellum, or marker paper to trace over these practice pages. If you don't draw directly on them, you can use them again and again.

Ready?

Upstroke

The first stroke is the upstroke, or entrance/exit stroke. It is commonly used to connect letters, as well as to start and finish them. To create this stroke, place your pen on the baseline and draw a very thin, light stroke upwards on an angle towards the waistline. Pressure should not be applied to your brush pen. Gently drag it up the page.

Downstroke

The second stroke is the downstroke, or full pressure stroke. To create this stroke, place your pen at the waistline and draw a heavy, thick line downwards on an angle towards the baseline.

Overturn

The third stroke is the overturn. It is used in miniscule letters such as *m* and *n*, and a longer variation is used for *z*. This stroke can be created by placing your pen at the baseline and drawing a light and thin stroke upwards towards the waistline, before turning over to the right and transitioning into a thick downstroke, finishing back at the baseline.

Underturn

The fourth stroke is the underturn. It is used in miniscule letters such *i, r, u, v,* and *w,* and a varied version is used for *t.* This stroke can be created by placing your pen at the waistline and drawing a thick, heavy downstroke towards the baseline, before turning under to the right and transitioning up into a thin, light upstroke, finishing back at the waistline.

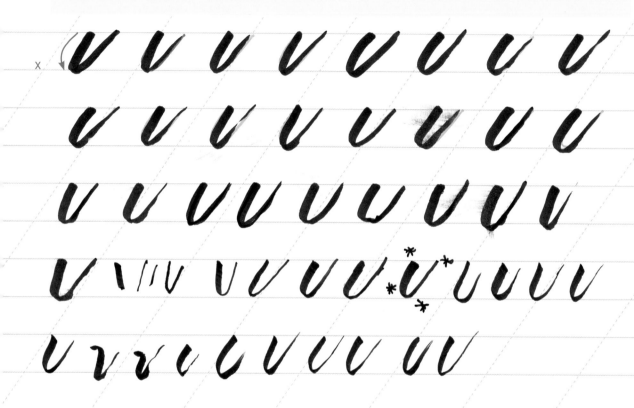

Compound Curve

The fifth stroke is the compound curve, which essentially combines an overturn and an underturn. It is used in miniscule letters such as *h, m,* and *n*. This stroke can be created by placing your pen at the baseline and drawing a thin, light upstroke towards the waistline, then transitioning over to the right and becoming a thick, heavy downstroke that heads back down towards the baseline. Without stopping, continue to transition back into a thin, light upstroke and take it up to the waistline. This should be one continuous stroke.

Left Curve

The sixth and seventh strokes are curves. The first curve is used in letters *c* and *e*, and can be used in place of an oval for letters *a*, *d*, *g*, and *q*. This stroke can be created by placing your pen about two thirds of the way up between the baseline and the waistline. Begin by lightly drawing an upstroke towards the waistline, curving over to the left. Transition down into a thick curved shape, then transition back to a light upstroke, finishing about one third of the way up between the baseline and the waistline.

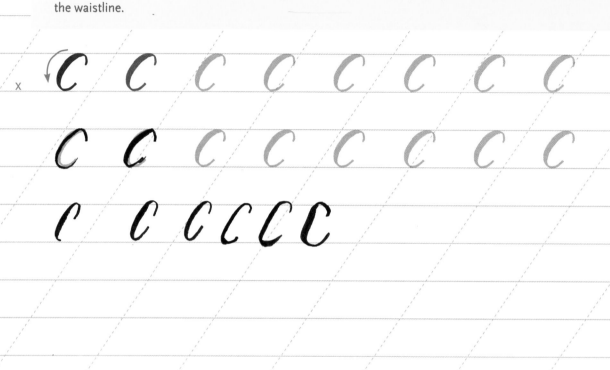

Right Curve

The right curve is a mirror image of the left curve and should follow the previous instructions, but be drawn in the opposite direction. It is used in miniscule letters such as *b* and *p*.

x

Oval

The eighth stroke is the oval. It is used in miniscule letters such as *a, d, g, o,* and *q*. This stroke can be created by following the instructions for the left curve stroke, but completing the oval by continuing the final upstroke until it connects with the beginning of the shape. This shape should always be created at about "2 o'clock on the clock" rather than at the top, because if the stroke begins as a heavy downstroke at the top, it is impossible to seamlessly connect the thick stroke with a thin stroke. It is much easier to connect two thin upstrokes.

Ascending Stem Loop

The final three strokes are all loops. The first loop is used as a stem in miniscule letters *d*, *f* (connected to the third loop), *h*, *k*, and *l*. (However, *d* and *l* do not finish on the baseline. Instead, they curve up into an underturn.) Begin by placing your pen on the waistline or just above, and drawing a light upstroke. Curve up and around to the left, and transition into a thick downstroke, finishing at the baseline. This stroke should pass through the first ascender but should not touch the second ascender.

Descending Left Tail Loop

The second loop is used in miniscule letters such as *g, j, p,* and *y*. Place your pen at the waistline and draw a thick, heavy downstroke that transitions at the bottom and curves to the left, continuing up towards the baseline as a light upstroke. This stroke should pass through the first descender, but should not touch the second descender.

x

Descending Right Tail Loop

The third loop is a mirror image of the second loop. It is used in miniscule letters *f* and *q*. In *f*, the first loop is connected to this third loop as one stroke. To create this loop, place your pen at the waistline and draw a thick downstroke that transitions at the bottom and curves to the right, continuing up towards the baseline as a light upstroke. This stroke should pass through the first descender, but should not touch the second descender.

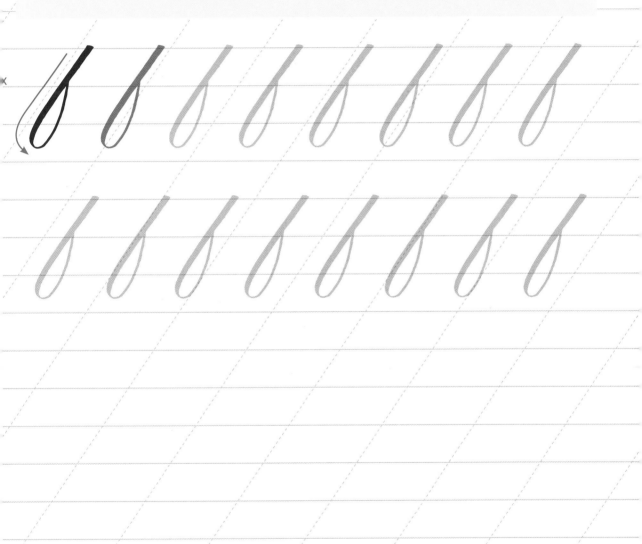

LEARN THE RULES LIKE A *pro* SO YOU CAN BREAK THEM LIKE AN *artist*

— UNKNOWN

the alphabet

Now that you've got a solid understanding of the staple strokes, it's time to start connecting them to form miniscule letters!

Connecting Staple Strokes

One of the biggest lightbulb moments for new brush letterers is realizing that each letter is made up of similar basic strokes. It can be intimidating to start a new art form, but once you see that the staple strokes you've just learned can come together and make the majority of the letters in the miniscule alphabet—what a relief! Suddenly, learning brush lettering isn't such a monumental task.

In the instructional pages that follow, you will see the miniscule alphabet broken down into the strokes you've just practiced. You will see which strokes go together for each letter, and the order and direction in which they should be drawn, just in case you need a quick refresher!

You'll then have a couple of light gray letters to place smooth paper over and to trace, and then some blank space to try drawing the letters yourself.

But before we get into that, let's have a look on the following pages at some common staple stroke connections, and what to look out for and aim for.

Upstroke (Entrance Stroke) + Oval (or Left Curve)

This combination will be used quite often, such as with *a, c, e, d,* and *g.*

While we have a set of "rules" for drawing staple strokes, it's important to remember you can bend them! For example, if we were to draw an entrance stroke from the baseline to the waistline (which you just learned to do) and then connect it with an oval or curve, it would look really odd. The entrance stroke would go higher on the guide sheet than where it first connects with the oval or curve. The way to get around this is to shorten the length of the entrance stroke. Instead of taking it up to the waistline, halve the size and finish it somewhere between the baseline and waistline. This will mean that when you draw the oval, the left side of the oval will connect smoothly in the middle.

Upstroke (Entrance Stroke) + Ascending Loop

This combination is used for letters *b, h,* and *l.*

A trap I see many beginners fall into is that they practice their staple strokes, then move on to letters and *completely* forget the staple strokes. I know you know what letters look like, but it's really important to slow down and stick to the "rules." Many beginners reach letters like *b, h,* and *l* and instead of drawing a separate entrance stroke connected to an ascending loop, they draw both strokes in one swift movement. Though this may seem efficient (and it's something you could incorporate further down the track when you're ready to stylize your letters), it's important not to do that now while we're focusing on consistency.

Here are some examples of what can go wrong if we don't "break" the line and draw each stroke separately:

Overturn + Overturn (or Compound Curve)

When we draw the letters *m* and *n*, there will be a bit of repetition. For instance, miniscule *m* is an overturn, plus an overturn, plus a combination stroke (which has an overturn in it). Miniscule *n* is similar, but shorter. When we are drawing letters that have repetitive strokes in them, it's important to aim for consistency. Focus on ensuring that all the overturns look the same. Are they on the same slant? Are you transitioning from thick to thin in the exact same place? Is there the same amount of negative space in each stroke? ("Negative space" is empty space. For our purposes, the white of the paper is negative space.)

Oval + Underturn (or Ascending Loop)

For miniscule letters such as *a*, *d*, and *g*, we need to connect a stroke with a straight line (such as an underturn or an ascending loop) to the oval that makes up the body of these letters. With these particular letters, the stroke with the straight line will be drawn on the right-hand side of the oval. The most important thing to remember when drawing the straight line stroke is to make sure you're not cutting off the oval in any way. Try to draw it next to the oval so the stroke *just* touches the oval's side. We don't want to change the shape of the oval by drawing over it. We just want the strokes to touch.

Upstroke (Entrance) Stroke + Underturn (or Descending Loop)

This combination is used for letters such as *i*, *j*, *p*, and *y*. If we are drawing the miniscule *i*, for example, we connect an upstroke with an underturn. Both the upstroke and the end of the underturn feature a light, thin line. Focus on keeping the thin upstrokes consistent. The upstrokes should both be drawn in exactly the same direction and on the same angle. With miniscule *i*, it's also important to ensure the downstroke part of the underturn is on the same angle as the two upstrokes.

General Notes about Connections

Try not to draw over strokes. Connect each stroke at the edge, instead of drawing over the stroke before it.

Remember to break the line. Letters that have loops should not be drawn in one fell swoop, but instead broken down into their individual strokes.

Aim for consistent shapes. If you're lettering a word and it has two of the same letters, or letters made of similar staple strokes, try to get them looking as consistent as possible. Take the word "big," for example. It has a *b* and a *g*, which both contain loops. Although one loop is ascending and the other is descending, it's important to ensure both loops are the same size and on the same angle.

Keep an eye on negative space. Look at your letters as shapes, and focus on ensuring the shapes match throughout the word. If a word has an *a, d,* and *g* in it, try to make the oval in each letter look the same. Check that the negative spaces in the loops of *d* and *g* are the same, and so on.

Rules are made to be bent. Although this book is full of rules, sometimes they must be bent. Think of the miniscule letter *l.* We need an upstroke (or entrance stroke) to begin it, and then an ascending loop—but wait a minute! That loop will not end abruptly on the baseline like the other ascending loops! No, instead we must curve the bottom of it around to the right, and create an exit stroke. The same thing happens with miniscule letter *d.*

Additional Strokes

Here are some other strokes you'll need to know. You'll see them in the next section.

Miniscule Letters

Seeing all the miniscule letters on one page can make it easier for beginners to understand just how often the pen needs to leave the page, as well as helping to identify the staple strokes that appear throughout the alphabet. In the examples on the next page, I changed pen colors with each new stroke, to show the stroke breakdown.

The way these letters are displayed shows you how they would look if they were in the middle of a word. Each letter has an entrance and exit stroke, so that you can see how it would connect to the next letter. It's not always necessary to connect letters, and some combinations look odd and clunky (more on that later). But it is helpful to know how to connect them.

I tend to avoid using entrance strokes when the word begins with a curved letter like *a*, *c*, or *e*. The entrance stroke on these types of letters looks a bit strange. However, I do prefer using entrance strokes on letters that have a thick downstroke after the entrance stroke, like *b*, *h*, and *l*.

Take a look at the miniscule letters all together, then practice each letter using the guide sheets ahead.

Note: These guide sheets are designed for small brush pens. To get larger brush pen sheets, visit www.blackchalkco.com/blbookextras.

a b c d e f g

h i j k l m n

o p q r s t u

v w x y z

· MINISCULE LETTER GUIDE SHEETS ·

Letter a: entrance stroke (ending in the middle of the x-height) + oval + underturn

x ‚ o v a a a a

x a a a a a a

x

x

Letter b: entrance stroke + ascending stem loop + right curve + exit stroke

x

x

x

x

52

Letter d: entrance stroke (ending in the middle of the x-height) + oval + ascending stem loop that curves around instead of ending abruptly

x　　ㆍ　o　l　d　d　d

x　d　d　d　d　d

x

x

Letter e: entrance stroke + varied left curve that starts in the middle of the x-height, curves up and around from right to left, continues down and around, and continues up to the waistline

x ℓ e e e e e e

x e e e e e e e

x

x

54

Letter f: entrance stroke + combination of the ascending stem loop and descending right tail loop + exit stroke

X

X

X

X

Letter g: entrance stroke (ending in the middle of the x-height) + oval + descending left tail loop + exit stroke

x

x

x

x

Letter h: entrance stroke + ascending stem loop + compound curve

X

X

X

X

58

Letter j: entrance stroke + descending left tail loop + exit stroke + dot

Letter k: entrance stroke + ascending stem loop + small loop followed by an amended underturn (shape looks like the right-hand half of a bow)

x

x

x

x

Letter l: entrance stroke + ascending stem loop that curves around instead of ending abruptly

X

X

X

X

Letter o: entrance stroke + oval + comma dot

Letter p: entrance stroke + descending left tail loop + right curve + exit stroke

x

x

x

x

Letter q: entrance stroke + oval + descending right tail loop + exit stroke

Letter r: entrance stroke + short varied comma dot that starts above the waistline and finishes on the waistline (before curving around like a traditional underturn) + underturn

X

X

X

X

Letter s: entrance stroke + s-shaped stroke that starts above the waistline and bends around to the left + exit stroke

X

X

X

X

Letter x: varied compound curve where the two thin upstrokes should be parallel to the 55 degree angle + another 55-degree upstroke to cross through the middle

x 𝒩 / 𝒩 𝒩 𝒩 𝒩

x 𝒩 𝒩 𝒩 𝒩 𝒩 𝒩

x

x

Letter y: entrance stroke + underturn + descending left tail loop + exit stroke

Letter z: overturn + varied descending left tail loop + exit stroke

Variations

You may find that you just don't *like* some of the letterforms I've shown you. And that's fine! Truth be told, I don't use the basic letterforms all the time either—they're just the foundation we need to set in place before we move on to decorating and getting fancy with our letters.

This section covers some letter variations you can try if you don't particularly love some of the basic forms.

Miniscule Letters r and s

Basic   Basic

Above, I've shown the basic letterform for miniscule *r* and *s*, followed closely by some common variations you can substitute. Letters with loops look more casual and whimsical, and can also be used to break up monotony and add a bit of fun to your words.

Miniscule Letters v and w

Below are the loopy versions of *v* and *w* you can substitute to add a little somethin' somethin'.

Basic   Basic

Miniscule Letters b and p

Basic

Basic

The alternate versions above for *b* and *p* are really similar, and involve changing up the letter's final stroke, which connects it to the next letter. Instead of rounding the letter out and connecting the exit stroke separately, simply create the final stroke as a loop.

Miniscule Letter t

Basic

I personally love the letter *t* because you can do so much with it, simply by playing around with the crossbar. See above for a basic *t*, wavy *t* (left to right), wavy *t* (right to left with some pressure at the beginning), and a super swashy *t* (left to right).

Majuscule Letters

Ah, majuscule letters! The ones that hardly anyone talks about or practices or draws because they are too confusing and hard, and it's way more fun to just use miniscule letters—am I right?

There's nothing frightening about majuscule letters! Yes, they are a little bigger (so you need to remember whole arm movement now more than ever), but they also have several key strokes in common, just like the miniscule alphabet.

In order to keep our majuscule letters as consistent as possible, we still want to use guide sheets! Majuscule letters use the top 3 boxes most of the time (x-height, 1st ascender, 2nd ascender). Most majuscule letters "sit" on the baseline and extend upward from there. There are a couple of letters that extend to every space in the grid. We won't be using the 55 degree slant for these, as their form lends itself more to a flowy and whimsical look, rather than rigid and structured like our miniscule alphabet.

NOTE: *These are my versions of majuscule letters. Just like the miniscule alphabet, there are no set rules when it comes to how your letters look! These are simply the majuscule letters I've come to love after months of research and practice, and ones that I've been able to incorporate some similar strokes into, to make them easier to learn. As with anything in this book, if you find a version you like better and want to incorporate into your style to make it yours, GO FOR IT!*

Take a look at the majuscule letters on the following pages and note how they sit on the grid. Then practice each letter using the guide sheets ahead.

About the Strokes

Unlike miniscule letters, majuscule letters don't have a set of agreed-upon staple strokes that form their building blocks. So instead of breaking them into staple strokes, I've demonstrated the stroke order a little differently. In the worksheets, the two colors show you how the letters are broken down. Each color change represents lifting the pen or a new stroke.

x

x

x

x

x

x

x

x

x

x

x

x

x

x

x

x

x

x

98

x

X

x

x

x

x

X

Evaluating Your Work

A great skill to develop during your learning journey is self-evaluation. It can be so easy in the beginning to draw a bunch of shapes or letters and think, "that sucks," or, "I hate that." While knowing whether something appeals to you or not is a decent start, it's even more important to recognize why you don't like it. Why are you unhappy with that particular stroke? Why don't you like the way that letter came out? Once you can figure out the "why," you can work towards a solution.

The easiest way to self-evaluate is to review your practice sheets. Say you've done a full page full of underturns. Pretend you're marking your own schoolwork, and go back with a red pen and tick the ones you think you nailed. Use them as your examples moving forward, and put a little question mark or a cross above the ones you don't like. Then it's time to figure out why.

Are the strokes angled in different directions, instead of being parallel? Is the transition between thin and thick strokes staggered instead of smooth? Is the end of the stroke flicked, instead of mindfully drawn all the way to the end? By recognizing what you don't like about what you've created, you can effectively move towards fixing it. The next time you draw the stroke or letter, you will have those comments in the back of your mind, and will be able to focus on correcting it as you go.

If you're having consistent difficulty with your technique or materials, and you can't seem to shake it, check out the Help section on pages 154–158 for advice on common brush lettering problems!

forming words

Connecting Letters

Connecting letters can be tricky. More often than not, we simply combine the exit and entrance strokes of two miniscule letters, and *voilà*! They connect perfectly. But when it comes to letters that have comma dots, or double letters, things can start to look weird and out of balance. Sometimes the best answer is not to connect the two letters at all!

Let's take a look at some different options.

Miniscule v and e

People looove to ask about this combination, because they looove to write the word "love." *V* and *e* can be really tricky, though! Above are some options you can try. First is the basic connection, which looks a little off because of the comma dot. Second is a variation that involves bringing the comma dot down so it connects more smoothly with the start of the *e*. Third is a wild, swashy version that doesn't connect. Finally, we have another basic version, without a connection.

Miniscule o and r

Another set of letters that can look a bit funny connected are *o* and *r*. When people begin lettering, they often love to try the loopy versions of letters, and *o* and *r* is a perfect example of TOO many loops! Some different options are above. The first two are basic connections that just involve changing the position of the comma dot in the *o*. The third variation shows a very loopy *o* with a basic *r*. Finally, we have a variation that involves no connection.

Another tricky situation is *double* letters. This is when we have two of the same miniscule letters next to each other in a word. Even worse: words that contain *multiple* double letters. Things can start to look weird, repetitive, or just a bit plain. But luckily there are plenty of ways to tackle this situation.

Miniscule s and s

First, we can connect the two letters in their most basic forms. Looks a bit odd, eh? A fun way to mix this up is shown in the second option, which involves one regular-sized s and one that's *much* bigger. Changing the proportions is a fun way to make a boring word look more interesting and sometimes more balanced. The third option incorporates two variations of the same letter. Lastly, as in previous examples, don't connect the two at all!

Miniscule r and r

Ahhhhh, "r & r." But this type of r and r is frustrating at first, not relaxing! The basic form of the letter r probably differs from the one you learned in school, which can make words look weird enough as it is—let alone when it sits right next to another r in a word! Just like in the s example, above are some ways you can mix up the letters r and r.

In general, remember to combine the entrance and exit strokes of the letters, as below, rather than simply placing them next to each other with their own individual entrance and exit strokes.

Correct

Incorrect

Spacing

Spacing is a key part of brush pen lettering that can make or break a piece of art. Legibility is crucial, and can sometimes come down to how much space you allow between the letters. **Minimum** is a great word to practice spacing with because it has SO many repetitive strokes. Not only do you get a thorough muscle memory work-out, but you also have to wrestle with the fact that some words can become *really* hard to read if you don't adjust the spacing. When you follow the correct letter proportions but end up with an illegible word, spacing can help you fix it.

minimum

minimum

As you see in these examples below, a word can change drastically just by adjusting the spacing. The first example looks very upright and formal. The second one becomes a little more relaxed, and the final one takes on a whimsical look as we increase the spacing and the slant.

Always keep legibility in mind when creating words. Your lettered artwork will make a much greater impact if people can read it.

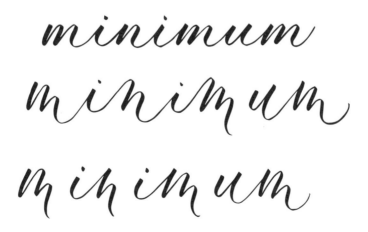

numbers and symbols

If you thought majuscule letters were rarely covered in the lettering world, don't get me started on numbers and symbols! These bad boys are rarely discussed in detail, yet are important, especially for people who want to address envelopes. Symbols are used less often, but it's still worth learning how to create them, in case you ever need them!

Again, these are just basic forms to get you started. I encourage you to change things up and do it differently!

As with the miniscule and majuscule alphabets, I've created a set of numbers with consistent shapes and strokes to make them easier to learn, and to give them a coherent overall look. Boom! Now you can address envelopes to your heart's content.

1 2 3 4 5 6 7 8 9 0

But what if we want to ask something, accentuate something, use it for social media, or just write a fancy ampersand? Let's look at symbols!

There are heaps of symbols (just look at your keyboard), but we're going to cover five common ones: the exclamation mark, the question mark, the pound sign / hashtag, the "at" symbol, and the ampersand.

! ? # @ &

About the Strokes

The two colors show you how the numbers and symbols are broken down. Each color represents lifting the pen or a new stroke. Practice each number and symbol using the guide sheets ahead.

1 1 1 1 1 1 1 1

2 2 2 2 2 2 2 2

X 3 3 3 3 3 3

X 4 4 4 4 4 4

5 5 5 5 5 5

6 6 6 6 6 6

x   7 7 7 7 7 7 7

x   8 8 8 8 8 8 8

x

?

x

x

• EXTRA PRACTICE PAGE •

advanced Techniques

Layouts

Creating layouts for lettering work is probably one of the most difficult things beginners encounter. There's no set of rules that you must follow, which is great, but also overwhelming. Here are some things I take into consideration when planning a layout.

Size

How big is the piece? Will it be on A4 paper? A huge wall? Will it be portrait or landscape? How will that affect the layout?

Shape

What shape should the piece be? Setting a boundary for yourself is helpful when deciding on a layout. It will give you something to work within, rather than running all over the page.

Emphasis

What part of the quote is important, or should be attracting the attention of viewers? Quotes have plenty of filler words (think: the, of, and) which can be minimized in size and relegated to the background. Say your quote out loud. Did you emphasize any words? Are any words important? If so, think of ways you can make them stand out the most.

Color

Will you be adding color to the piece, or will it be monochromatic? Are the colors you've chosen compatible, or will they clash and disrupt the piece?

Audience

Who is the piece for? Are you designing something for display in a public space where people might not know how to read calligraphy? Be mindful to make your piece very legible if it is being viewed by people who aren't familiar with lettering. Take it easy on the flourishes as well.

Use Pencil

Save yourself time, money, and stress by planning your layout with pencil. Draw the boundary we talked about, write your emphasis words nice and big, and start to play around with how you can fit the rest of the words in.

Mix It Up but Be Consistent

There's nothing wrong with combining multiple styles of lettering to add interest to a piece, but be sure you stay consistent within those styles. Think: repeating the same flourishes. (For more on flourishes, see page 128.)

Ask a Friend

This is something I do *all* the time. I always check my layouts with my team or friends if I'm not 100 percent in love with them. Sometimes a fresh set of eyes may be all you need to solve something that was bugging you, or to offer a helpful suggestion that will improve the piece.

Working on a Layout

Let's say I want to create a layout for the quote, "Create something every day even if it sucks."

There are a few options when it comes to which words to accentuate. Maybe the word "create" should really stand out, because that's what the quote is all about: creating.

Or maybe "every day" should stick out more, to highlight the importance of doing something regularly.

Or maybe highlighting the word "sucks" will grab people's attention with a mild "shock factor."

Below, I've set the boundary rectangle and started to sketch the piece out, accentuating my key words and noting any space that needs filling later:

I've also added in some lines for "create" and "sucks" to follow. They run in different directions to create interest. Those are the words I've chosen to accentuate.

I've then de-emphasized "something every day" and "even if it." I might use different colors or a different style, and add serifs onto the block letters. (For more about block letters, see page 130–132.)

I've also noted the negative space. I might use this area to create some kind of illustrated design in the middle, so that it breaks the piece up, or a flourish. The corner under "sucks" also looks a bit blank. It's not quite the same in the top near "create" because of the swashes on the letters. The *t* fills in that space nicely. A swash on the bottom of the *k* could fill this space. (For more about swashes and flourishes, see page 128.)

Taking all this into consideration, I created the final lettering below. I changed the angle of the word "sucks" for legibility.

The sketch on the previous page is very basic, but I hope that it has illuminated the kinds of planning that go into a successful layout. We can create dynamic layouts in so many different ways: boundary shape, color, lettering style, accentuated words, illustrations, and more. The sky is the limit.

Negative Space

Negative space (or blank space) has been touched on earlier in this book, regarding the empty space within shapes and letters. But what about negative space between words? So glad you asked!

When students start creating layouts, I notice the same problem again and again. (It's natural, by the way. No shame in it.) I see them drawing words exactly as we've learned throughout this book, and not breaking away from traditional shapes. Students are hesitant to add illustrations or flourishes, and it creates big areas of negative space.

negative space

Too much unbroken negative space within a design can throw it off balance. Rather than looking like a beautiful piece of work centered around amazing lettering, it just looks like a bunch of words stacked on top of each other.

Don't be afraid to judge your own work. Judge it hard! Being your own worst critic can help you if it means you're critically assessing your own work for improvement. So take a look at your finished piece, and figure out where you can improve it. Have you left too much space between the words of a quote you've written? Is one side full of loops, making it off balance? Could you add some flourishes or illustrations to balance it all out and create visual interest?

Crayligraphy

A term you'll come across in the brush lettering world is *Crayligraphy*, which means calligraphy created using a Crayola marker. Cool, huh?

You might not think it by looking at them, but the cone-shaped tips of Crayola markers can create a brush lettered effect. The technique differs, however, because unlike a traditional brush pen, the Crayola tip doesn't flex—meaning it doesn't respond much to pressure. You'll need to rotate the angle as you draw in order to get both thin and thick strokes. This is actually a great habit to get into, because it will also help you make the most of your traditional brush pens!

If you hold your brush pens at an upright angle, no matter how hard you press, you will only be able to get so much of the brush tip in contact with the page. (That's also really bad for the tip in general!) However, if you adjust your grip, holding the brush pen a little farther back so that it's closer to parallel to the page, you will be able to touch almost the entire long side of the brush tip to the paper, creating a beautiful thick downstroke. But if you maintain this angle the entire time, it will make achieving a thin upstroke quite difficult because too much of the tip will be touching the page, even with hardly any pressure applied.

You can solve this dilemma by rotating the angle as you go. Getting the hang of it will take some time, but it will mean you achieve the thinnest possible thin strokes, and the thickest possible thick strokes. When you draw a downstroke, make sure the brush tip is low to the page so that the majority of the brush tip touches the paper. As you transition from a heavy downstroke to a light upstroke, lean the pen angle more upright as you start releasing pressure, so that you only touch the very tip to the page.

This technique is best learned using a Crayola conic-tipped marker. Why? Because you won't achieve the brush lettering effect with them otherwise! As mentioned earlier, these markers don't really respond to pressure, so you will be forced to "roll" the marker from its flat side onto its pointy tip as you go in order to get a thick and a thin stroke. Not only that, but it will prevent you from destroying your actual brush pens if you practice this technique on something cheaper and more rigid like a Crayola.

Getting into this habit early will set you up for greater success down the road, but it does take time to master, so hang in there!

Bouncing Baselines

As you begin to master the basic letterforms from this book, you will no doubt start wondering: How can I get my letters to look fun and flowy like all the ones I've seen?

Enter: bouncing baselines.

Bouncing is a term given to lettering that doesn't follow a straight line (like the grids you have been using in this book so far). Instead, it has a fun bouncy or jumpy look to it, with letters sitting at different heights and the sizes of individual letters varying.

Some beginners really struggle with breaking away from the basic letterforms. It's no surprise when people like me are drilling guide sheets into your heads!

For some people, however, this is an easy thing to achieve. For those of us in the "this is hard" camp, there are a couple of things you can do to help.

Firstly: Stop using guide sheets! Immediately stop using a straight baseline. I dare you to draw in a straight line now! *Double dare* you.

Often this isn't enough, so another thing you can do is draw yourself a wavy or bouncy baseline, and follow that curved shape around instead.

This will force you to conform to a new shape. However, it can still look quite structured, so the next thing you can do is start playing with individual letters on that bouncing baseline.

One super easy way to create a bouncy effect with your letters is to take anything with an ascending or descending loop and make the loops really big. Think: descenders like *g*, *j*, and *y*. Really exaggerate the loops. You can do a similar thing with ascending loops (such as *d*, *h*, and *l*), but they are a little trickier to flourish, as you start with the loop instead of finishing with it. However, simply making the loops bigger can have a fun and bouncy effect on your lettering.

I also have a general rule of thumb that you may want to follow: I keep my vowels relatively small. This is just something I have always done, and I find that it helps with legibility. However, I do like to play with the letter *o*, and exaggerate its top loop.

The other thing you can do is bring down your connecting strokes beyond the baseline. Up until now, for the most part you have been connecting your letters by taking an exit stroke from the baseline up to the waistline, then connecting to the next letter. Now that you are breaking all the rules, try taking these connecting strokes lower.

I love to do this with letters that are still easy to read, such as any of the descending looped letters or *f*, *k*, and *t*. Legibility always needs to be the top priority, and playing with certain letters (such as *c* or *u*) can make them look like other letters, creating confusion for readers.

Flourishing

After bouncing, the next technique beginners want to try is flourishing.

A flourish has traditionally been described as a separate piece of the design (not attached to letters) that creates interest in a piece, and fills negative spaces. It's usually a flowy or curly line, and can be made using the same pen as your lettering. However, these days the term "flourish" is often used in place of "swash," which is when a flourish is attached to a letter.

For simplicity, I will use "flourish" or "flourishing" to describe any fancy hand-drawn curls and swirls.

Balance is the most important thing to keep in mind when flourishing. Beginners are often unsure where to flourish, and this confusion can result in unbalanced pieces or unnecessary flourishes.

When I look at words, I see a pattern. I look at the shape of the letters as a design, and imagine how I can balance the piece out using flourishes.

Think about the word "lettering." It has a tall letter at the beginning (*l*) and a long descending letter at the end (*g*). This is already a pretty balanced word. That doesn't mean we can't add to it, just that we should be careful not to unbalance it.

If I were approaching this word, I would exaggerate the sizes of the *l* and the *g*, to make their loops large and dramatic, and add a flourish to the loop of the *g*. I can balance this out by using a majuscule *L* instead of a miniscule *l*.

Then comes the issue of the double *t*. Seeing as I have already dramatically increased the loop of the *g*, I can balance this out by adding a fancy flourish to the crossbar of the *t*.

If I hadn't gone so wild with the *g*, I probably would have remained more conservative with the double *t*. Keep balance at the top of your mind!

When it comes to adding flourishes that aren't attached to letters, the main rule is not to cross two thick lines together, as that creates a very heavy and clunky look. We still want to follow the same thick downstroke, thin upstroke rules. But before intersecting two lines in a flourish, be sure you have tapered the line off so that you aren't crossing a thick with a thick.

There are no hard and fast rules about which letters you can and cannot flourish, or how you must flourish them, so take some creative license! Play around with different letters and different shapes, and create a catalog of go-to flourishes in case you ever get stuck. I've included some of my favorites below to get you started.

• DIFFERENT ALPHABET STYLES •

Ready to try new alphabet styles? Check out the following pages for inspiration!

Plain Block Letters

A B C D E

F G H I J K

L M N O P Q

R S T U V

W X Y Z

Serif Block Letters

A B C D E
F G H I J
K L M N O
P Q R S T
U V W X
Y Z

A B C D E F
G H I J K L
M N O P Q
R S T U V
W X Y Z

Flowy Miniscule Script

a b c d e

f g h i j

k l m n o

p q r s t

u v w

x y z

Blending

Blending brush pen colors is a fun technique that can be done in a few ways. The best types of pens to use for blending are those with water-based inks such as Tombow and Ecoline. These pens are designed to be blended with other colors in their range.

Tools:

- Paper
- Two or more brush pen colors
- Blending palette (optional)
- Blending pen (optional)

Note: Some brands sell blending palettes (fancy version of a piece of plastic) or blending pens. You don't need these to be able to blend, but you're welcome to try them. Blending pens are colorless pens that you can either draw directly onto the tips of, or swipe them through colors you have placed down on plastic. A substitute for the blending palette is a plastic lid or sandwich bag.

Technique #1:

- Using a darker shade of brush pen, put color down onto a blending palette or piece of plastic.
- Using a lighter shade of brush pen, "pick up" the darker color on the tip of the lighter color.
- Draw away and watch the beautiful blending effect!

Technique #2:

- Using a darker shade of brush pen, draw directly onto a lighter shade of brush pen, being careful to only rub the tips in one direction (up and away) so as not to fray them.

Technique #3:

- Use a colorless blending pen to try the first two techniques. Draw directly onto the blending pen with other colors, or use the blending pen to "pick up" other colors from a blending palette or piece of plastic.

Technique #4:

- For brush pens that aren't specifically designed for blending and shouldn't have other colors applied to them (e.g. Artline Stix), use a waterbrush to blend two colors together. By using a waterbrush to mix the colors, you won't stain or permanently affect the color of your pens.

Technique #5:

- Ecoline has created pots of ink that mix perfectly with their own brush pens. Take a brush pen (pink or blue is best) and dip the tip into a pot of ink (again, pink or blue is best—whichever one isn't the color of your brush pen).

Remember to clean your pens by simply drawing strokes on a page until the darker color no longer appears. If you are using a colorless blending pen, you will notice that even when the colors stop showing up in pen strokes, the pen may be stained.

Ombré Effect

You can create a pretty gradient effect with your lettering by simply applying and releasing pressure on your brush pens. This technique has been called the "ombré effect" and is most easily achieved when using pens that dispense a lot of ink (such as the Artline Stix or Ecoline brush pens) on very smooth paper.

Tools:

- Smooth paper
- Inky brush pens
- Your hand!

Technique:

- Your downstrokes need to be quite heavy. It's surprisingly easy to *not* achieve this effect. The more pressure you apply, the more ink is "squeezed" out onto the page.

- Smooth paper will give you the best possible result. Using absorbent paper will mean the gradient effect is harder to see. We want the ink to sit on the paper, not soak in.

- Your upstrokes need to be very light, barely touching the paper so minimal ink comes out.

- If the gradient isn't as obvious as you would like, carefully draw over the top half of your letters to make them darker. You could even use one shade of brush pen darker if you wanted to create a dramatic effect.

- Remember to always use your brush pens on an angle. Never apply heavy pressure to them in a vertical position, as it will damage the tips.

FAQ: Won't you damage the pen by doing this?

Not if you're using smooth paper and have the pen on an angle! It can seem wrong to press so hard you cause the pen to squeak, but you will not damage or fray the pen if you're using high quality smooth paper with the pen on an angle.

Highlights

Adding highlights to your lettering is a fun way to create depth and really bring your words off the page.

HIGHLIGHT

HIGHLIGHT

Tools:

- Paper
- Brush pens for initial lettering (Darker colors will make the highlight more obvious.)
- Opaque white pen or ink (Uniball Signo is a personal favorite. Dr. Ph. Martin's bleedproof white ink works too.)

Technique:

- Letter your chosen word.
- Decide which direction the light source will come from.
- Using the white pen or ink, draw a line, dot, or half square in the corner(s) facing the light source.
- Success!
- Remember that the highlights should be facing the light source! Shadows do the opposite, and we'll cover those next.

Shadows

Adding shadows is another fun way to create depth with your lettering. You can do this in a variety of ways, but my favorite is using a gray marker (to look all shadow-y) or a monoline pen.

Tools:

- Paper
- Brush pens for initial lettering
- Gray brush pen or black monoline pen to create the shadow (but feel free to experiment with a range of colors!)

Technique:

- Letter your chosen word.
- Decide where the light source will come from.

- Using the gray brush pen or the black monoline pen, outline the sides of the letters that are OPPOSITE to the light source.
- Success!

- Try to visualize something real when you do this. If you had a box sitting on a table, and a light shining on it from the top left, where would the shadow be cast? To the bottom right! So if we imagine the light source on our lettering is at the top left, we need to outline the bottom and right sides of our letters.

Stippling

Another way you can fancy up your letters is stippling. This is a technique where little individual dots are drawn to create shading and dimension. A good way to use this technique is to draw a letter or word in a light color, then add the stippling in either a darker shade of that color or black.

You could also reverse it and draw a dark color, then use a metallic or white opaque pen for the stippling! It's a pretty time-consuming effect, but it looks super fun, doesn't it? Especially combined with that ombré!

Wherever you choose to add the dots (bottoms or tops of letters), be sure to concentrate them in one area, fading them out as you go. If you apply dots all the same distance apart, or over the entire letter, it won't have the same dimensional effect.

Illustrations

Illustrations are a fun and easy way to add something extra to your work. Whether it be a banner, some florals, or even a couple of stars, a little embellishment can make a piece really eye-catching.

Here are some super simple examples to try for yourself. For ideas about where to add illustrations to your lettering, see the **Layouts** section on page 120.

Combining Styles

You started off this book by learning the basics, but the end goal is to really make brush lettering your own. It's super important to have a solid foundation from the beginning, but if no one did anything but the basics, our lettering would all look the same and it would be pretty boring.

COMBINING styles

Now that you've seen a range of techniques, it's time to start playing around. These techniques lead to lots of "happy accidents," and will help you develop your own style.

One of the easiest ways to find your own style is to combine multiple types of lettering in a piece. This might be as simple as using block letters with flowy script. Maybe it involves adding illustrations, or blending. Play around and see what works. You will at least discover what you *don't* like, which will help you find things you *do* like.

I am a huge fan of combining block letters with script. It's easy, and it can really make a design pop. There is such a thing as too much flowy script, and sometimes it needs to be broken up with block letters, which really assist with legibility.

Try combining as many styles into one piece as you can. See what happens!

Finding Your Own Style

Teaching brush lettering to others is an interesting balance between demonstrating what people want to know (my style) and helping them learn what they need to know (the basics).

While it's perfectly normal to admire someone else's work, the cooler part is that *you* could develop your own unique style! I bet there are a bunch of artists whose work you recognize instantly. Wouldn't that be cool if it happened to you?

There's no instructional manual for developing your own style. It takes time and a *lot* of experimentation.

Take a look at the world around you. Check out book covers, store signage, graffiti. Inspiration is everywhere, and you never know what you'll find. Every now and then I'll see a new way a particular letter is drawn, and before I know it, it has been incorporated into my style.

The biggest piece of advice I can give you is to stay curious. Look at the world around you, research, go to workshops, talk to people about art, be inspired. Most of all, stick to it, even when you feel like you're not making any progress. Keep showing up, practicing, and learning, and your style will find you.

Brushes with Bristles

Once you feel comfortable using regular brush pens, I encourage you to try a brush with bristles—either a regular paintbrush, or an aqua brush.

I encourage students to get the hang of regular brush pens first because brushes with bristles require much more control. Not only do you have to remember all of the other things you've learned in this book so far, but you then have to control the pesky little bristles that splay out all over the place. Lettering with bristle brushes is much easier to pick up once you already have experience with brush pens.

There are a few brands of brush pens that come pre-inked and have bristles. I found this tool hard to get the hang of when I started, but now I know how to work it!

Bristle brushes are great for lettering with pots of ink such as Ecoline. The colors are vibrant and mix beautifully. They can also be used with regular watercolor paint, for either painting or trying some watercolor lettering!

Watercolor Lettering

Watercolor is such a fun activity, and can really take your lettering to the next level.

Not only can you use water brushes for lettering with watercolors and expanding your palette, but you can also experiment with new mediums, including masking fluid, gouache, and my favorite, metallic paints.

The great thing with bristle brushes is that you can use them to create lettering on watercolor paper. It is definitely not recommended to use your brush pens on watercolor paper, especially if it is cold press or rough, as the surface will destroy your pen. That's not to say I haven't done it, though! So now you have an alternative. Fancy lettering on a gorgeous watercolor background? Yes, please!

what next?

Sharing Your Work

One of the best parts about learning brush lettering will be the people you meet! Most of us don't start "arting" with the intention to make a bunch of new friends, but for some magical reason, the lettering community is absolutely buzzing with kind, supportive, and encouraging people.

They won't just show up at your house, though. You need to seek them out!

Some of the best people and most amazing opportunities will come to you via social media, so I highly encourage you to get out there and share your art. There is a thriving community of artists on Instagram, and they welcome newcomers with open arms.

I know it can be scary to put your name or face to your artwork, and you definitely don't have to in the beginning. I sure didn't! But you'll find if you open yourself up and are happy to share your wins and your losses, your successes with art and your failures, you will attract an awesome tribe of other creatives who will want to see more and more of your work.

Two years ago I never would have thought that creating pretty letters would be my job. Had I not joined Instagram and shared what I was doing, none of this would have happened! That's pretty crazy to think about, but goes to show how worthwhile it is to share your work.

Another great place to post your art is on a blog or website. Having an online portfolio will allow people who will pay for your artwork to find and contact you. If that's not your aim, you can still have a website full of your beautiful work. One of the greatest ways to meet new people and make friends is by sharing what you know, and discussing art related issues with the community. A blog is great for this.

Finding Other Creatives

Instagram isn't the only place creatives hang out, though! You'll find a handful of good groups on Facebook that have great conversations about art supplies, techniques, and troubleshooting.

It's also highly likely that your city has a calligraphy society. Search online!

Lettering and calligraphy are becoming more and more popular, meaning more and more events and workshops are popping up all the time. No one is ever too experienced to learn, and I always encourage others to go to as many workshops and take as many classes as they can. Even if the content is similar, every teacher has a different way of teaching. You're guaranteed to find other creatives at a creative workshop!

Continual Improvement

There's one sure-fire way to continue to improve, and that is to continually practice! No one ever became good at anything by just thinking about it or hoping. You must put in the time.

If we go back to thinking about muscle memory, it makes more sense. How can we expect our body to memorize all these strokes if we're not training it? It's like sports. If you don't flex your muscle memory, you won't perform on game day.

It's not a race, though. And you should avoid comparing yourself to others and their level of skill at all costs. Some of us only have time to practice two or three days a week after the kids go to bed, while others (like myself) can do it all day every day. Naturally, those with more time to practice will likely excel faster, but that doesn't make them more skilled or better.

Even a few minutes a day will help you, and the early stages are critical to building that muscle memory. Once you're a bit more experienced, you can put your pens down for weeks and still be able to use them perfectly when you choose to pick them up again. But it's all about getting to that level first.

Attend as many workshops as you can, not just to meet other creatives, but to stretch your mind by trying new things. When it comes to art, there's always something new to discover!

This doesn't have to break the bank. There are a ton of cheap and even free websites, videos, and tutorials that will teach you all about art. Start off on Instagram, check out YouTube, and get yourself over to Pinterest. Inspiration is in the palm of your hand. (It's also outside, and you should go there too.)

Further Resources

If you're interested in finding other people with as big a passion for pens as you, as well as staying in the know about upcoming lettering-related events and workshops, and want to receive a bi-monthly dose of knowledge and inspiration and articles from other artists in the lettering community, check out *Penultimate Magazine*. I founded this magazine in 2017 with the mission to create, educate, and collaborate.

I also co-founded the Instagram page Letter Archive (@letterarchive), which I encourage you check out! It is full of inspiration for individual letter styles, and showcases amazing work from talented artists and everyday pen friends from our community. Sometimes a dose of inspo is all you need.

projects To Try

On the following pages are some things I've done with brush lettering, from murals, to café signage, to lettering on mirrors, to fancy wine and liquor labels, to place cards, to hand-lettered ornaments. Take a look and start dreaming up ways to letter your world!

149

help

• MATERIALS TROUBLE •

Don't freak out! It's not you, it's the materials. Here are the two most common issues with supplies and what to do about them.

Frayed Pens: What the Fray?

Have you noticed one of your brush pens has gone "fuzzy" and isn't drawing lines as crisp as it used to? Or perhaps the brush tip has become a lot softer and more difficult to control? Sounds like you've become a victim of the dreaded fray!

What is fraying?

Fraying is when the tips of brush pens become damaged. This prevents them from performing as they should. The damage can usually be seen if you look close enough, with the brush tip appearing fuzzy with bits of roughed-up fabric sticking out to the side.

What causes fraying?

More often than not, improper use of brush pens causes fraying. This could be from using rough paper (printer paper or card stock are notorious frayers), applying incorrect pressure (heavy handed on both upstrokes and downstrokes, or applying heavy pressure while the pen is positioned vertically), or simply from overuse. Brush pens don't last forever!

How can I prevent fraying?

The best way to avoid fraying is to always ensure you are using smooth paper with your brush pens (unless you absolutely must use rough paper, and are happy to sacrifice the life of your pen). Also, only apply heavy pressure during a downstroke, and keep your pen on roughly a 45-degree angle to the page when doing so. There is no way to 100 percent guarantee your pen won't fray. It is inevitable! We can certainly slow down the process, though.

What do I do with a frayed pen?

BURN IT. Just kidding, that's not safe. You can either throw it away and replace it, or use it for brushier-looking scripts! I personally love the look of textured lettering from frayed pens, or from those running out of ink—they're both perfect for that effect! Another great purpose is to use them for practice. Why waste the ink of a perfectly good pen when you could be drafting designs with a frayed pen? You're welcome!

Bleeding Paper

Have you noticed ink bleeding into your paper? Take it to the ER, STAT! (Also kidding.) If the ink from the brush pen you're using is seeping outwards from your lines and into the fibers of the paper, you may not be using the best type of paper for brush lettering. Bleeding ink can also be frustrating, as our lines lose the crispness they should have, giving our letters a fuzzy appearance.

I always recommend smooth paper for brush lettering. Being so smooth also means the ink "sits" on top of the surface, rather than seeping in and bleeding like it does on regular copier paper. Ink sitting on top of the page means we can do fun things like the ombré effect!

Rougher paper types are the ones that tend to aid and abet bleeding ink, and if you remember from earlier, we want to avoid rough paper at all costs! Though it's pretty, textured paper isn't really a good fit for brush pens, so try to find something smooth that has a coating on it, which will prevent the ink from bleeding. Rhodia, tracing paper, or vellum are good options.

Technique Trouble

Okay, so it's not the materials, it's you. Here are some common issues with technique and how to overcome them.

Shaky Lines

One of the most common cries for help from beginners is that their lines, particularly their upstrokes, are shaky—and they just can't shake it! I hate to break it to you, but this will likely be a problem you face *forever*! Intermittently. But forever.

Shakiness is just a part of brush lettering and calligraphy. Some days we are on our A-game, and other days we are out of touch. This is why practicing drills is so important. By building strokes into muscle memory, they become more effortless. Drills are commonly used by professional calligraphers as a warm up exercise, so please don't think they are just for newbies! Think about it; if you had one chance to do a project, such as lettering people's names on a marriage certificate, would you jump straight in? Or would you spend some time warming up and practicing what you're going to write? Exactly. However, practicing drills still won't prevent you from ever getting the shakes again. Sorry!

There could be a few other reasons your lines appear shaky. Maybe it's your wobbly hand! Are you cold, nervous, caffeine-deprived, or the opposite? Sometimes simply standing up, taking a break, and shaking it out can help.

Have you been trying to letter with your hand hovering above the table? Your hand should be resting ON the table, but lightly. Let your hand and arm lightly graze the top of the table as you move. If you hold your hand and arm *off* the table, you will find it extremely difficult to maintain control and consistency. If you plant your hand and arm in one spot, you will restrict your movement. By letting them lightly slide over the table, you'll keep your lines more consistent but allow yourself the freedom to move and create longer strokes.

You may also be thinking too hard. Sometimes we place too much pressure on ourselves to get something perfect, and end up concentrating far too hard on getting it right instead of just letting loose and going with the flow. Try to loosen up your death grip on the pen, remember to engage your whole arm, and don't forget to breathe!

Thick Upstrokes

Not seeing a huge difference in thickness between your upstrokes and downstrokes? Let me help!

Are you using a frayed pen, like we just talked about? Perhaps your much-loved brush pen has seen better days and the tip has worn out. This could be the reason behind the not-so-thin lines! I'm not saying go out and replace all your pens, but just be mindful that new pens have crisp tips and haven't been "worn in" yet, whereas pens that you've used a lot can soften and eventually become very difficult to achieve thin strokes with.

Mind the G.A.P.! Don't forget the three main principles: grip, angle, and pressure. If your upstrokes are looking like your downstrokes, you may be gripping the pen too close or too far back, preventing you from getting the thickest of thick strokes and the thinnest of thin strokes. Refer back to the Crayligraphy section (page 124) for how you can improve your technique.

Angle also plays a big part. For downstrokes, be sure you're using your brush pen on its side, not with the end of the barrel pointing towards you. We want to get as much of that brush tip on the page as possible!

Or maybe you're being too careful? Most brush pens (Artline Stix in particular) love heavy pressure, so don't be afraid to push down! Simply creating a thicker thick stroke may be enough to give you a nice contrast against your thin strokes.

Have you tried turning your page? Some people can letter perfectly in a horizontal straight line (who are you and where did you get these magic powers?), but most of us need to turn our page on an angle to achieve the best results. Try rotating the paper and see if it makes a difference. Just make sure you don't skew your body in the process. That won't be good for your posture. Move the paper, not yourself!

Transition Issues

Drills seem like fun and games until we have to connect a thin and a thick stroke! Here are some ways you can overcome transition issues between two different strokes.

Take it SLOW! Lettering fast is a no-no (at least in the beginning), so my biggest tip is to make sure you are taking your time with your strokes. The slower you go, the more time you have to control the pressure you apply and release on your pen. If you rush your strokes, you don't have the ability to correct any errors as you go. By taking it slow, you create this opportunity. If you think you're already drawing slowly, I challenge you to go even slower. Don't be fooled by the time lapse videos online!

Eyeball your work. I see a lot of beginners mindlessly draw their letters, then look back at them and hate them. Instead of powering ahead, as above, slow down and watch what you're doing closely. This will help you see mistakes as they're about to happen, and will let you adjust.

Frayed pen? A well-loved or frayed pen may be causing you transition issues. The softer and squishier our brush pens get, the harder it is to control them during transition strokes. Try swapping it for a different or new pen and see if that makes a difference.

Inconsistency

We've talked a bit about consistency already, but if you're having trouble getting your letters to look the same, check out these tips:

Don't flick the ends of your strokes. This is a common habit that a lot of people have from their handwriting style, but it is not conducive to lettering. Ensure you're drawing very slowly, finishing off your strokes as slowly as you started them.

Engage your whole arm. Effective lettering involves using your *whole* arm! Hand lettering is not handwriting, and despite that fact it's called "hand" lettering, you need to engage your entire arm in the process. Focus on the motion and the power coming from your shoulder. Make sure you don't have arm rests or anything else restricting this movement. To achieve long and consistent strokes, you need the range of motion that only your whole arm can provide.

Keep using guide sheets. Guide sheets are the easiest way to keep your letters consistent. The quicker you build the correct movements into your muscle memory, the quicker you can ditch them!

Watch your work as you go. Rather than lettering a whole word and getting to the end only to hate it, pay attention to what you do as you're doing it. Eyeball your work. If you drew a loop at the start of your word and there's one at the end, look back at the first one before you draw the second one so you can aim to create the same size, shape, and angle.

Evaluate your work. The best way to improve is to know where you're going wrong, and why. If you're not happy with something you've drawn, figure out why.

Change pens. Sometimes we stick with the same pen for too long in one sitting, and it just doesn't work for us. Occasionally all we need is a fresh pen, and everything falls into place. Be sure that the pen you're using isn't worn, either, as that could contribute to inconsistency problems.

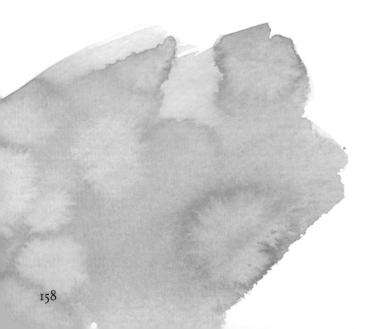

acknowledgements

To my students and fellow penthusiasts from all over the world, thank you. Without you, this wouldn't be a thing. I so very much appreciate the continued support, and I love sharing this art form and passion for pens and pretty letters with you.

Jen, Nathan, Ally, Becca, Rachel, and Nikki—your friendship, support, encouragement, jokes, and advice never go unnoticed or unappreciated. Thank you all for the important part you play in both my personal and professional life (and for keeping me sane, most of the time).

Lastly, a huge thank you to my ever-so-patient and encouraging editor Talia Levy, and the team at Peter Pauper Press, for seeing the potential of this book and asking me to share my passion with the world.

about the author

Emma Witte is the Founder and Chief Pen Wizard of Black Chalk Collective, a modern calligraphy and lettering studio based in Melbourne, Australia. Artistically talented as a child, Emma put down the pens and paper for many years while she made her way through school, university, and the corporate world. In late 2015, Emma spontaneously attended a brush lettering workshop, and thus a love affair was born. Combining her new obsession with pretty letters, business, and humor, Emma formed Black Chalk Collective and now dedicates much of her time to teaching others how to unleash their inner artist, all while having a bit of fun. To further enable her obsession with lettering and sharing what she knows, Emma also runs a pen-focused bi-monthly publication, *Penultimate Magazine*. Emma is a firm believer that anyone and everyone can create beautiful art with just a little time, patience, and perseverance.